THE WORLD'S FINEST COLLE
OF BRITISH CERAMICS

Staffordshire has long been the centre of Britain's pottery industry. Here at The Potteries Museum & Art Gallery we have the very finest collection of British ceramics in the world with which to tell the story of the potters' art.

The first museum collection in the Potteries began as early as 1828 and the number of pots has been growing ever since. Many of our most important pieces have been given or left to us by local people, some of whom were pottery factory owners, such as Alderman Thomas Hulme, Percy W.L. Adams and the sanitaryware manufacturer Thomas W. Twyford. Other pieces have been given to us by collectors who were not from Staffordshire but who loved pottery, the museum and its collections. Two important collections of studio pottery have been donated to us in this way: one in 1948 by Dr Henry Bergen and the second in the 1990s by Robert Pinchen.

We have also acquired pots for the museum with the help of gifts, grants and donations. These include whole groups, such as the Pugh collection of Staffordshire portrait figures, which was bought in 1980–81 and, more recently, study collections of the well-known author on ceramics, Dr Geoffrey Godden. Many special, individual pots have been bought over the years, including one of our most famous exhibits, Ozzie the Owl.

Until the Second World War (1939–45) there were five small museums in the six towns which now make up the City of Stoke-on-Trent. At the outbreak of war the smaller museums closed and their collections were moved to the countryside for safety. After the war Hanley Museum & Art Gallery became the central museum but it soon became clear that the Victorian building was too small to house all the collection. As a result, Stoke-on-Trent became the first local authority after the war to build a new museum. It opened in 1956. This new building (on our present site) was only the beginning of the project and in 1974 building began on the Museum & Art Gallery as it is today. It was opened by HRH The Prince of Wales in 1981 and won the Museum of the Year Award in 1982. In 1998 it was renamed The Potteries Museum & Art Gallery in honour of the industry which gave this district its name.

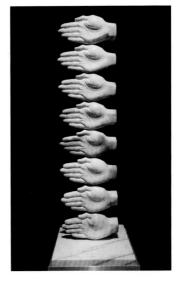

▲ 'Hands' by Glenys Barton, 1983; commissioned by The Friends of the Potteries Museums & Art Gallery to commemorate the museum winning Museum of the Year in 1982.

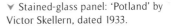

▼ Stained-glass panel: 'Potland' by Victor Skellern, dated 1933.

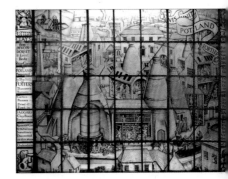

SMALL BEGINNINGS:
POTTERY IN MEDIEVAL BRITAIN

In the Middle Ages there were small potteries wherever suitable clays could be found within reach of a local market. Fuel was also needed and pots were fired using wood, or in Staffordshire, coal. Throughout the country, potters used different clays, fuel and kilns, so pottery varied, giving distinctive types from each area.

Shapes were mainly functional and included jugs, cooking pots and serving dishes. Decoration was less important than function and could be simple clay modelling, coloured clay slips or lead-based glazes. Lead gave a very glossy surface and the addition of copper gave a green colour. In addition to being decorative, potters realised that glaze could make a pot watertight.

Other products of the medieval potter were floor tiles, made for use in abbeys, churches and palaces. These were decorated with coloured glazes, by moulding, or by inlaying patterns in clay of another colour into a basic red clay tile. These were made by travelling tile makers who moved from building site to building site as required.

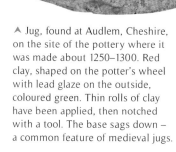

▲ Jug, found at Audlem, Cheshire, on the site of the pottery where it was made about 1250–1300. Red clay, shaped on the potter's wheel with lead glaze on the outside, coloured green. Thin rolls of clay have been applied, then notched with a tool. The base sags down – a common feature of medieval jugs.

Black ware was red earthenware covered with a lead glaze which was rich in iron. This was made from about 1600 into the early 1700s. Drinking vessels such as mugs and multi-handled tygs were the forms most commonly made.

Mottled brown glazed, buff earthenware was coloured by the addition of manganese to the lead glaze. It was made from the 1680s until the 1760s.

Midlands yellow ware describes light-coloured earthenware which was glazed with lead and fired to a honey-yellow colour.

Midlands purple ware was unglazed red earthenware fired at a higher temperature, giving it a purple-brown shade. In Staffordshire, this was made from about the late 1400s into the early 1700s. Storage vessels, such as butter pots with a maker's mark stamped on them, have survived from the late 1600s.

Slipware was decorated lead-glazed earthenware. Its popularity put the Staffordshire Potteries on the map from the 1640s.

▲ Medieval tile: earthenware with impressed design with contrasting slip added. Made in the 14th century, probably Staffordshire.

◄ Early Staffordshire pottery
1680–1747: iron-glazed tyg and mug.

▲ Henry Sandon and friend.
Ozzie the Owl appeared out
of a bag during filming of the
BBC's *Antiques Roadshow* at
Northampton, for a programme
broadcast in 1990. Ozzie was later
sold at auction and purchased for
the museum. The piece was one
of Henry Sandon's best 'finds' in
his years with the television series.
Ozzie was made in Staffordshire
around 1700; the body and head
form a jug and cup which have
been decorated with coloured clay
slips to look like the feathers and
features of an owl. The head and
body were thrown and modelled,
then thick, liquid clay slip was
applied to the surface. More clay
slip was then trailed and dotted on
and the colours swirled together.

➤ A slipware dish made in
Staffordshire in the early 18th
century continues the owl theme:
press-moulded and decorated with
a slip-trailed owl surrounded by
owlets.

A WISE MOVE:
STAFFORDSHIRE SLIPWARE

Slipware is one of Staffordshire's most distinctive types of pottery and
large quantities were made for about a hundred years from the middle
of the 1600s. It was sold all over the country and exported abroad, even
as far as America and the West Indies.

Staffordshire potters used local buff and red clays to make their
ware, and then decorated it with liquid clay (or 'slip') before coating
it with lead glaze. Clays and coal for fuel were plentiful, and a skilled
workforce was established which meant that Staffordshire rapidly
became the most important pottery-making district in Britain. For
this reason the pottery industry grew up and remained in North
Staffordshire, even though white-firing clays and other raw materials
were brought from other areas as the manufacture of more refined
wares replaced slipware in the 18th century.

The majority of slipwares were decorated
simply with dots, lines or feathered
patterns but some were much
more elaborate, often made
to commemorate special
events. Many of these
more decorative
pieces are now in
museums. Some
of the slipware
potters' names are
known because
they included
them in their
elaborate designs:
Thomas Toft is
perhaps the most
famous of all.

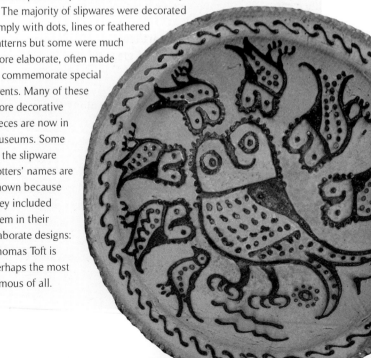

SLIPWARE: A LONG TRADITION

Decorating earthenware with coloured liquid clay ('slip') has a long tradition. In the late 1500s British potters, inspired by wares imported from Europe, began to make slipware. Somerset, Devon and Kent were some of the first districts where slipware was made, but by the 1640s it was being produced in Staffordshire. At the end of the 17th century it was being made at potteries all over Britain.

By the 1720s Staffordshire potters began to move away from making slipware using local clays, so some of the traditional slipware potters moved to areas where there was still a demand for their skills, such as Shropshire, Bristol and West Cumbria. Slipware production continued in rural areas such as Devon and Yorkshire, and it is still made today by some studio and craft potters.

▼ Harvest jug with sgraffito decoration and the inscriptions 'God bles King George And All his Men And send Admerell Vernon home Again' and 'Drane by me Thomas Stonman June 27 Made by me Edward Reed GI7R4I'. Made in North Devon, 1741.

Making slipware

Slipware pots were made in several ways: they could be thrown on a wheel, moulded or slab-built from sheets of clay. Press moulding, where a sheet of clay was pressed over a mould of the desired shape, was a popular method of making dishes from the mid-1600s.

The most common method of applying slip decoration was by trailing. This was done by mixing clay with water and sieving it until it was smooth and runny. Trailing tools were made from cows' horns or pottery. The slip was put into these tools and poured out in a stream through a hole or quill nozzle. Better effects could be made by covering the surface of the pot with slip before starting to decorate it. This provided a more even surface and allowed combed or feathered patterns to be made. Several slips of different colours could be used to create elaborate designs with outlines, dots, areas of colour, trellis patterns and inscriptions.

If the slip covering the pot was allowed to dry out it could then be scratched off to reveal a different coloured clay beneath. This type of decoration is known as 'sgraffito'.

◄ Dish with a slip trailed design of a gentleman and the name of the potter, Thomas Toft. Made in Staffordshire, about 1670.

TIN-GLAZED EARTHENWARE

The skill of making tin-glazed earthenware, sometimes called 'Delftware', was brought to England by Dutch potters in the late 1500s. In this process, red or buff earthenware was given a coating of lead glaze which was made opaque and white by adding tin oxide to it. Decoration was painted onto the powdery white surface before the pot was fired. Chinese porcelain was much admired at the time, and the patterns on tin-glazed earthenware often imitated Chinese designs.

Tin-glazed earthenware was never made in Staffordshire. It was made in ports such as Bristol, London, and Liverpool where raw materials, such as tin for the glaze, were easily imported. Tiles, useful wares for barbers and apothecaries, and elaborate, decorative pieces were made from tin-glazed earthenware but it was not very durable, and from the mid-1700s other, stronger pottery replaced it.

▲ Posset pot with slip trailed decoration which includes the inscription 'THE BEST IS NOT TOO GOOD FOR YOU 1696 RF'. Made in Staffordshire, 1696.

▼ Cradle with slip-trailed decoration and the inscription 'made by Ralph Shaw October the 31 Cobridg:gate MT 1740'. Shaw came from a well-known family of Staffordshire potters.

▲ This huge punchbowl in tin-glazed earthenware, 50cm across, features a painted scene depicting several views of a ship, a sloop named *Nanny*. It was decorated for the *Nanny*'s owner and captain, George Dickinson, and was made in Liverpool, where the ship was built. The bowl was probably painted by John Robinson at James Pennington's factory and was ordered before the *Nanny* set sail in November 1767. Unfortunately the bowl was never delivered, as George Dickinson and his ship were lost at sea off the West Indies in 1769. The bowl was presented to Hanley Mechanics Institute around 1828, by Enoch Wood who acquired it from John Robinson after he moved to Staffordshire around 1770. It was one of the first pieces to be acquired for the museum.

STONEWARE: INDUSTRY IN ACTION

Salt-glazed stoneware

Much more durable than tin-glazed earthenware, salt-glazed stoneware was developed in Europe, firstly in Germany in the late Middle Ages, and came to Britain during the 1670s. At first it was made by the Thameside potters of London, but later it spread to Nottingham, Derbyshire and many other areas including Staffordshire.

The most common type was brown stoneware, which was used widely for domestic pottery and other useful wares into the early 20th century because of its strength and durability. Decoration was often moulded in relief: hunting and drinking scenes were popular, as were simple designs and inscriptions incised or impressed into the soft clay before it was fired. Clays were usually grey or buff-coloured when fired and could be given a warm brown colour with iron oxide. The glaze was made by throwing common salt into the kiln during firing, where it vaporised in the high temperature and settled on the surface of the pots. The process gives a characteristic surface that is rather like orange peel.

⋏ Salt-glaze saggar. Pots were fired in saggars, fireclay boxes which protected them during firing and meant the kiln could be well stacked. Normally saggars had solid sides and were placed on top of each other to seal the open tops, but for salt-glazing they had large holes in the sides so that the salt could settle on the surface of the pots once it had turned to vapour in the heat of the firing. This saggar is from a failed batch – the mug inside is firmly fused to the base and sides. It was made (and discarded) at Burslem, Staffordshire, during the early 1700s.

Red stoneware

During the 1690s, two Dutch brothers named Elers came to Staffordshire and created fine red unglazed stoneware, made by slip-casting and decorated with applied moulded patterns. They were inspired by Chinese red stoneware teapots, imported into Britain by the East India Company. The Elers did not stay long in Staffordshire and were very secretive about their methods. It was not until the 1740s that local potters began making red stoneware again, using established methods of throwing, turning and relief decoration. The red clays used could be fired at such a high temperature that they became impervious to liquids without the need for a glaze. Red stoneware tea and coffee wares grew in popularity as these drinks became common during the 18th century. Later in the century, stoneware came to be made in increasingly sophisticated and fashionable styles and in colours other than rich red, including brown, buff and black.

◁ Mug: slip cast red stoneware, made in a mould, decorated by turning on a lathe and with applied floral sprigs. Made by the Elers Brothers at Bradwell Wood, Staffordshire, about 1695.

Salt-glazed stoneware in Staffordshire

In the early 18th century Staffordshire potters perfected the methods of making white salt-glazed stoneware, and it was the

➤ Teapot: white salt-glazed stoneware with painted decoration in overglaze enamel colours. Made in Staffordshire, 1755–65.

success of this which spread Staffordshire's reputation for pottery making and exporting world wide.

White-firing clays from Devon and Dorset were combined with crushed and calcined flint from Kent to produce a fine white body. Moulds were used extensively to produce complex shapes and decoration, so potters were able to move away from the traditional range of round shapes made on the thrower's wheel. Some shapes were copied from other materials, such as silverware with elaborate rococo decoration. Another new development was the production of items not previously made in pottery, such as spoons, and teapots in unusual shapes, including houses, ships and animals. Many plain, undecorated wares were made, but more expensive items had painted, printed, or incised and coloured decoration.

Oriental porcelain remained popular on the tables of the wealthy throughout the 18th century, but from the 1720s affordable, decorative and practical wares were made in Britain and were available to more people than ever before.

Fine earthenware took over from salt-glazed stoneware in popularity in the 1770s, but not before large quantities had been made and sold, bringing great prosperity to the Potteries.

▲ Loving cup: white-salt-glazed stoneware with scratch blue decoration, including the inscription '1754 EB'. The design was incised into the surface of the pot before firing and cobalt blue pigment rubbed into the lines. Made in Staffordshire, 1754.

▲ Mug: buff salt-glazed stoneware, covered in white slip, with an incised design and the inscription 'E:W 17:23', filled in with iron brown slip. Made in Staffordshire, 1723.

◄ Punch pot: white salt-glazed stoneware with overglaze printed and painted decoration including a portrait of Prince Charles Edward Stuart; decorated in support of the Jacobite cause. Made in Staffordshire, about 1755.

▼ Brown salt-glazed stoneware teapot and small mug, both excavated in Burslem, Staffordshire. Made in Staffordshire, about 1710.

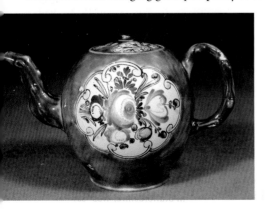

EARTHENWARE IN THE 18TH CENTURY

In 1715 there were about 500 pottery workers in north Staffordshire, but by 1785 this had increased to around 15,000. The industry took off during the 18th century, as new techniques of making, decorating and firing led to better, cheaper pottery for the ever-increasing market at home and abroad. In particular, raw materials from the south of England, such as flint from Kent and white-firing clays from the West Country, became vital. White salt-glazed stoneware was made from these clays, but they could also be used to make fine, light, lead-glazed earthenware.

Local Staffordshire clays, used for slipware and red stoneware, were also used to make lead-glazed red earthenware. From the 1720s and into the second half of the century these were sometimes decorated with moulded and applied relief decoration made from white clay. Another technique was to mix together different coloured clays to make pots with a marbled effect, known as agate ware. Black earthenware could be made from clay very heavily stained with iron oxide and with a lead glaze that gave a shiny black surface.

Creamware

During the mid-18th century, making porcelain was difficult and expensive, and few potters in Staffordshire attempted the task. They were concentrating on making an attractive and far cheaper alternative which had been developed by the late 1740s – creamware, a fine quality white earthenware.

At first, creamware was often decorated with simple patterns in green, yellow, brown and purple which were applied to the body before being fired with a clear lead glaze. Because of the effect this produced these are known as 'tortoiseshell wares'. By the 1760s and 70s, fashions had changed and creamware had improved so that the colour of the pottery itself became an important part of its appearance. By this time potters in other areas, such as Yorkshire and Derbyshire, had also began to make this very popular type of ware.

Decoration on creamware became more varied as technology progressed. Relief-moulding was used, sometimes with additional painted colours; green glaze, developed in the late 1750s, was used to create cauliflower- and fruit-shaped wares; hand-

▲ Cauliflower coffee pot: relief-moulded in creamware with green glazed leaves and clear glazed top. Made in Staffordshire, 1760–70.

▲ Loving cup: red earthenware with applied white sprigged decoration. Made in Staffordshire, 1740–60.

painted overglaze enamel colours became very popular from the 1760s; and the new technique of transfer-printing gave rise to a whole range of commemorative, humorous and pictorial scenes.

Famous potters

There are many famous potters' names which have become linked with different types of pottery in the 18th century, often without good reason, but documentary research and archaeological excavations have given us a much better idea of who was producing what. It is clear that the thriving potter would produce all kinds of wares, very much like his neighbours.

Red earthenwares and stonewares of similar shapes have been excavated at various sites in Staffordshire, including Samuel Bell's works at Newcastle-under-Lyme and at sites in Hanley and Shelton. Enoch Booth of Tunstall is credited with technical advances in the making of creamware in the 1740s and some rare pieces have survived.

Thomas Whieldon was a leading potter in the 1750s and 60s. Excavations on the site of his pottery at Fenton, Staffordshire, have made it possible to identify some pots made there. Whieldon is famous for having taken on the young Josiah Wedgwood as his junior partner in 1754. Also potting at Fenton from 1762 to 1782 was William Greatbatch, whose products included a full range of earthenware and stoneware.

▲ Jug: creamware with sprigged and applied clay decoration, underglaze painted colours and the inscription 'RH 1757'. Moulded sprigs exactly matching these have been excavated from the site of Thomas Whieldon's works at Fenton, Staffordshire. This jug was possibly made by Whieldon for a Ralph Hammersley.

◄ Teapot: creamware with sprigged and applied clay decoration and underglaze colours ('tortoiseshell ware'). Possibly made by Thomas Whieldon at Fenton, about 1755.

► Jug: creamware, overglaze printed in black with 'Conjugal Felicity', the print signed 'Thos. Fletcher & Co. Shelton'. Made in Staffordshire, 1795–1820.

◄ Creamware teapot with enamel painted decoration. Sherds of this design were found at the site of Thomas Whieldon's factory at Fenton but may not have been unique to his works. Made in Staffordshire, 1755-65.

▲ Model of a dovecote, entitled 'A NEW PAVILION': creamware with underglaze colours ('tortoiseshell ware'). Made in Staffordshire, 1750–60.

▼ Dish creamware with relief-moulded decoration of fruit and nuts, and a repeated pattern in the centre: decorated with sponged underglaze colours. Made in Staffordshire, 1760–70.

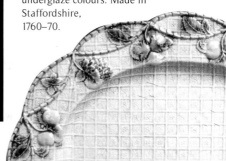

WEDGWOOD: ONE OF MANY

Josiah Wedgwood FRS FSA (1730–95): his epitaph in Stoke-upon-Trent church states that he 'converted a rude and inconsiderable manufactory into an elegant art and an important part of the national commerce'. While he was a leading figure in promoting the industry and the wares of the Staffordshire potteries worldwide, he was also one of a whole group of ambitious manufacturers in an age of progress.

When Wedgwood left his partnership with Thomas Whieldon in 1759 to set up his own factory in Burslem, the Staffordshire potteries were increasing in numbers and the variety of their wares was growing. Wedgwood was a brilliant potter, chemist and businessman. With the aid of his friend and partner, Thomas Bentley, he successfully marketed his wares to the wealthy and aristocratic classes.

Wedgwood's technical achievements included the perfecting of a fine green glaze during his partnership with Whieldon. He made great improvements in the production of creamware; in 1765 he presented Queen Charlotte with a tea and coffee service and was allowed the title 'Potter to Her Majesty'. He named his creamware 'Queen's Ware', a name still used by the Wedgwood company today. In the late 1760s he also improved basalt, a black unglazed stoneware inspired by ancient Greek pottery. Wedgwood's best-known invention, however, was jasper, a coloured unglazed stoneware with white relief decoration. Many experiments took place before it was made successfully in 1775.

In 1769 Wedgwood built a new pottery factory designed on the most modern principles, and named it Etruria. To supply power, the factory had its own

▲ Signature of Josiah Wedgwood from his apprentice indenture.

▼ Jasper vase with applied relief decoration of 'Hercules in the Garden of the Hesperides', impressed mark 'WEDGWOOD'. Made by Josiah Wedgwood at Etruria, Staffordshire, about 1785.

◄ Black basalt vase with 'encaustic' painted decoration of classical figures, impressed mark 'WEDGWOOD'. Made by Josiah Wedgwood at Etruria, 1769–1800. Wedgwood was inspired by Greek and Roman pottery, particularly items from the collection of Sir William Hamilton which are now in the British Museum, London.

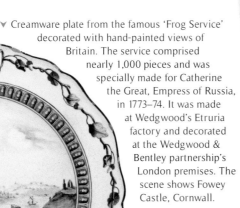

▼ Creamware plate from the famous 'Frog Service' decorated with hand-painted views of Britain. The service comprised nearly 1,000 pieces and was specially made for Catherine the Great, Empress of Russia, in 1773–74. It was made at Wedgwood's Etruria factory and decorated at the Wedgwood & Bentley partnership's London premises. The scene shows Fowey Castle, Cornwall.

windmill and, later, a steam engine. It was strategically placed on the Grand Trunk Canal (later the Trent and Mersey). Wedgwood was a partner in the enterprise to build the waterway, realising that canals were essential to successful trade in order to transport both raw materials and finished goods efficiently and cheaply.

Wedgwood was far from alone in his achievements. He had many successful rivals in Staffordshire and beyond. Fine jasper, basalt and other stonewares were made by Staffordshire potters such as the Turners at Lane End (Longton), Humphrey Palmer (followed by Neale & Co), and Elijah Mayer at Hanley, to name but a few. Large factories were established by other manufacturers, such as William Adams and Enoch Wood at Burslem. Josiah Spode, who had also worked with Thomas Whieldon, established his business at Stoke-upon-Trent in the 1770s; the name, like Wedgwood, continues today. In Leeds and other areas, important potteries were making high-quality wares which rivalled those of Staffordshire.

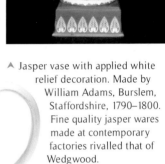

⌃ Jasper vase with applied white relief decoration. Made by William Adams, Burslem, Staffordshire, 1790–1800. Fine quality jasper wares made at contemporary factories rivalled that of Wedgwood.

➤ Teapot: creamware, with transfer printed and enamel painted decoration of 'The Prodigal Son in Excess', from a series illustrating the well-known Bible story. Made by William Greatbatch, Lower Lane (Fenton), Staffordshire, 1775–82.

⌄ Teapot: white stoneware with brown slip ground to panels and sprigged white ornament. Made by John (or John & William) Turner, Lane End (Longton), Staffordshire, 1800–10.

◀ Pearlware jug with underglaze blue decoration and the inscription 'Tidmarsh's Original Staffordshire Warehouse'. Possibly made in Staffordshire, late 18th century, by James Tidmarsh, Cobridge, for relatives who were dealers in pottery and glass in London. By this date many of the bigger Staffordshire factories had their own London warehouses.

CHINA COMES TO THE WEST: PORCELAIN IN BRITAIN

Chinese porcelain was much admired in Europe, and many attempts were made by western potters to make this beautiful and highly-prized material. The art and 'mystery' of its production was known in China for many hundreds of years before it was perfected in Europe in the early 18th century. In Britain, many potters were keen to follow in the footsteps of German and French factories such as Meissen and Sevres, where the complex process of porcelain-making was successfully mastered.

Early British porcelain

The ambition of British potters was to make true, oriental-style 'hard-paste' porcelain, but it was the middle of the 18th century before they began to make any kind of porcelain successfully. There were major early porcelain-making factories in London, Worcester, Derby, Lowestoft and Liverpool: Staffordshire's commercial success came late in the 18th century, despite earlier ventures. The first porcelain to be made in Staffordshire was produced in 1746 at the Pomona works, Newcastle-under-Lyme, but this was never marketed widely. There was more extensive production of tableware, ornamental ware and figures at Longton Hall a few years later, in the 1750s.

Most early English porcelain makers could produce only 'soft-paste' porcelain – imitation porcelain – but a few, at Bristol and Plymouth for example, continued to pursue the elusive secret of making true, hard-paste porcelain. The New Hall factory in Staffordshire was established in 1781 by a consortium of potters who saw the commercial possibilities of hard-paste porcelain production. One key to their success was the use of the correct type of clays from the huge deposits found in Cornwall. Although patent restrictions created some difficulties, porcelain-making became well established in the late 18th century and New Hall had many rivals.

Bone china: a very English invention

Although bone ash had been used to make soft-paste porcelain, at the Bow factory, London, for example, it was the late 1790s before it was discovered that fine, strong and very white porcelain could be made by using much larger quantities added to the other ingredients (mainly of china clay and china stone). Josiah Spode at Stoke-upon-Trent is said to have introduced bone china, but it very soon became the standard British porcelain type, made by

▲ This soft-paste porcelain plate has scattered floral and insect motifs in the centre to cover blemishes on the surface. In the early days, porcelain was difficult to make and the high failure rate made it very expensive. Made at Longton Hall, Staffordshire, 1750–60.

▼ Pair of soft-paste porcelain figures representing Autumn and Spring, made at Longton Hall, Staffordshire, 1755–60.

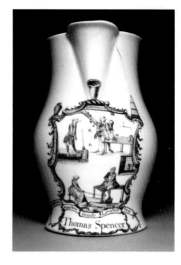

most porcelain manufacturers in Staffordshire and elsewhere. It was much admired abroad, but it remained a very British product.

During the 19th century, British porcelain swept the world. By the time of the Great Exhibition in 1851, it had become highly elaborate and technically sophisticated. The simple forms of the early decades gave way to the Victorian taste for complicated shapes in the style of earlier centuries, often with a great deal of gilding. Fine porcelain wares were produced for all pockets: technology had advanced to the extent that, by the second half of the century, inexpensive tableware could be made in huge quantities. At the other end of the scale, art on porcelain was popular, and skilled, highly paid artists painted landscapes, figure compositions and all kinds of subjects on to expensive ornamental wares. The work of artists at Derby, Worcester, Coalport, Swansea, Rockingham and the major Staffordshire factories was much admired, and remains so today.

⌃ Large tureen: bone china, decorated with hand-painted oriental scenes known as the 'Chinese Temple' pattern, chosen by the Prince of Wales in 1806. Made by the Staffordshire firm of Davenport, pottery- and glass-makers at Longport from 1794 to 1887.

⌃ Hard-paste porcelain teapot with an enamel painted pattern, No. 253. Made at New Hall, Staffordshire, about 1790–95.

> An exhibition piece: floral painting by the Continental artist C.F. Hürten on a bone china vase specially made by W.T. Copeland & Sons, Staffordshire, for the International Exhibition of 1871.

⌃ Bone china as 'canvas': a view of the Bay of Naples, painted and signed by Daniel Lucas, on a tray made in Staffordshire about 1850–60.

⌃ The enamel painted decoration on this porcelain jug shows scenes of pottery-making and the name of a Liverpool potter, Thomas Spencer, for whom it was made, possibly as a wedding present in 1764. Probably made by Richard Chaffers & Co, in business in Liverpool 1754/5–65.

> Botanical painting of an aconite on a Spode bone china dessert plate of about 1810.

WHO MADE THAT POT?

W.B. & Son Sylvan
This is a very informative Victorian mark, printed and impressed with the name and initials of the makers, William Brownfield & Son, a design registration mark for the pattern 'Wild Life in the Alps' issued 10 June 1875 and with an impressed date mark for May 1876.

Marks are put onto pottery in different ways and for different reasons. Many pots have none at all. Marks often include the name or initials of the maker, sometimes the factory name, the pattern, the date, or a worker's own mark. Sometimes a name may be that of a retailer, designer or special customer. Numbers on pottery are usually part of a factory's own record system and can include a pattern number, a date code, a shape number or a worker's number. Marks only became common in the late 1700s and more informative in the Victorian period.

Impressed marks: The simplest form of mark is made by pressing a tool into the soft clay pot before it is fired. The tool has letters, numbers or a symbol, like printer's type, which makes a neat mark which can be repeated on large numbers of pots. Impressed marks are amongst the earliest used in the pottery industry: they appeared from the 1760s and were quite common from the 1780s. They are still used today at some factories.

The name is usually the potter's surname, or a number or year symbol can indicate the date. Code systems such as design registration marks can be impressed.

Moulded marks: These marks are made as part of the making process of moulded pots, or are made in small, separate moulds and applied to the pot. They can be quite ornate and are also useful for marking identical pots in large quantities.

The potter's name and additional information such as a date or pattern number could be included. Design registration marks were often moulded at the same time the pot was made.

Printed marks: The earliest form of printed mark would have been engraved onto the copper plate along with the pattern. When the pattern was transferred onto the pot, the mark was applied to the base. The earliest printed marks were used in the middle of the 18th century and the method has continued to be the most popular for marking pottery.

Printing is a cheap and easy way of marking pots. Designs can be quite ornate, and in the 19th century a whole range of wreaths, arms and other decorative designs were used, often along with the maker's name or initials and possibly a pattern name. More recently, new methods of printing have taken over. Lithographs, rubber stamps and silk screen prints are used to mark pottery.

Incised marks: Like impressed marks, incised marks are applied when the pot is still soft. A sharp tool is used to scratch the name, words or numbers into the clay. This method of marking is not usually used for mass-produced factory products, but is more often found on craft pottery of the late 19th century onwards.

Painted marks: Painted marks are made by using ceramic colours on a fine brush. Blue was a common colour used under the glaze, but a wider range of colours was used over the glaze. Again, it is not a common method of marking mass-produced goods, but often expensive, hand-painted

Wedgwood & Bentley
An impressed mark on the back of a jasper plaque made about 1775–80, during the partnership between Josiah Wedgwood and Thomas Bentley.

Moulded mark
A moulded design registration mark for 20 May 1859 and maker's mark of William Brownfield, on a relief-moulded stoneware jug.

St Paul's Cathedral
Underglaze blue transfer-printed mark giving the pattern name, the manufacturers T. & J. Carey and their trade name, 'Saxon Stone China', used between about 1823 and 1842.

Adams Micratex Cookware
The wording indicates a late-20th century date – Adams used this backstamp between 1984 and 1987.

DESIGN REGISTRATION MARKS AND NUMBERS

Registration marks and numbers were used to protect the rights of the designer or maker. From 1842 to 1883 a diamond-shaped mark with coded letters and numbers could be printed, moulded or impressed onto pottery.

1842–67
year letter at top
A = 1845
B = 1858
C = 1844
D = 1852
E = 1855
F = 1847
G = 1863
H = 1843
I = 1846
J = 1854
K = 1857
L = 1856
M = 1859
N = 1864
O = 1862
P = 1851
Q = 1866
R = 1861
S = 1849
T = 1867
U = 1848
V = 1850
W = 1865
X = 1842
Y = 1853
Z = 1860

1868–83
year letter at right
A = 1871
C = 1870
D = 1878
E = 1881
F = 1873
H = 1869
I = 1872
J = 1880
K = 1883
L = 1882
P = 1877
S = 1875
U = 1874
V = 1876
W = 1878
(1–6 March)
X = 1868
Y = 1879

1842–83
months for both periods
A = December
B = October
C or O = January
D = September

(Diagram 1842–67: Class — IV at top; Year — X; Month; C, RD, I — Day of the month; 8 — Parcel number)

(Diagram 1868–83: Class — IV at top; Day of the month — I; 8, RD, X — Parcel number; Year; C — Month)

E = May
G = February
H = April
I = July
K = November and December 1860
M = June
R = August and 1–19 September 1857
W = March

From 1884 a simple number was issued, starting from 1 and reaching the following numbers each decade:

Date	Number	Date	Number
1.1.1890	141273	1.1.1950	860854
1.1.1900	351202	1.1.1960	895000
1.1.1910	552000	1.1.1970	944932
1.1.1920	673750	1.1.1980	993012
1.1.1930	751160	1.1.1990	2003711
1.1.1940	837520	1.1.2000	2090000

Two helpful books for finding out about marks are: G. A. Godden, *Encyclopaedia of British Pottery & Porcelain Marks* (Barrie & Jenkins) and J. P. Cushion, *Pocket Book of British Ceramic Marks* (Faber).

wares were marked in this way. A painted factory title or description of a painted scene could be given.

From the late 1700s the most commonly found painted marks are the numbers which factories gave to their patterns. These would relate to the pattern books held by the factories to assist in keeping records and for ordering wares. In some rare cases, pattern books have survived or a range has been identified from known designs, so it may be possible to identify a maker from a pattern number alone.

Words used in marks:

England, Made in England: From 1891 goods for the US market had to be marked with their country of origin. From the 1920s the wording suggested was 'Made in' the country of origin. This resulted in many marks from the 1890s onwards including these words whether or not they were intended for the US market.

Limited, Ltd: The first Limited Liability Company in the Potteries was registered in March 1861. Its use became more common in marks from the 1870s.

Ovenproof, Detergent and Dishwasher Safe, Microwave Safe: These are all quite modern phrases which indicate that the pots on which they are found probably date from the 1950s or later.

Turner's Patent
Painted mark in red overglaze enamel on a stone china plate made by J. & W. Turner. Their patent was taken out in 1800.

Pattern number 8184
The shape upon which this pattern number is painted. The high number itself identifies the maker as Samuel Alcock, about 1840.

15

FIGURES

▲ Lovers in an arbour: earthenware with underglaze colours and lead glaze. Made in Staffordshire, 1750–70.

Figure-making has been a part of the Staffordshire pottery tradition since the late 17th century. Amongst the first figures to be made were salt-glazed stoneware animals and people, including delightfully naive earthenware musicians in white and red clays. More elaborate arbour groups and pew groups were made in salt-glazed stoneware and tortoiseshell-coloured creamware of the type used to make tablewares. With their soft colours and simple modelling, these figures have a particular charm of their own.

During the second half of the 18th century, very elaborate porcelain figures were made at the major factories in London, Derby and the West Country, but the Staffordshire potters specialised in less expensive, more popular earthenwares. By the end of the 18th century their figures had become more colourful and accurate in detailing, and some show how they were copying styles made popular in porcelain.

Portrait busts of famous personalities of the day were made, often in large quantities, as in the case of John Wesley and Napoleon. The Staffordshire figure became an important record of history and social change in its own right. In the early 1800s, subject matter increased steadily and figures became yet more colourful and detailed. Biblical scenes and moral tales were depicted, with whole groups of figures on table-shaped bases or with modelled trees or 'bocage'.

▲ Polito's Menagerie: earthenware model depicting a well-known travelling circus that visited Staffordshire; painted overglaze enamel colours. Made in Staffordshire, about 1830.

The habit of applying marks became more widespread in this period, so particular makers can be identified in some cases. We know of the products of the Wood family of Burslem through documents once used at their factories; the names of the potters Salt and Walton are often found on the back of their figures, but by far the majority of figures remain anonymous.

Toby jugs

No one can say by whom or when the first Toby jug was made, but this type of jug in the form of a seated drinker has been made in Staffordshire since at least the 1780s. 'Good Sir Toby' may have been an actual historical figure, or he may have been a Shakespearean character, but he has inspired potters for over two centuries. Various models of Toby were made, including a female version, Martha Gunn, a bathing attendant in early-19th century Brighton. During the 20th century, character jugs depicting all kinds of fictional and real personalities were made, particularly by the Staffordshire firm of Royal Doulton, whose bone china figures, often of ladies in period dress, also became very popular.

◄ Toby jug: a toper seated on a barrel in earthenware with underglaze colours. Made in Staffordshire, 1785–1800.

A HERD OF COWS AND A CROWD OF FROGS

Drinking tea, coffee and chocolate became popular in the 18th century and tablewares were needed to serve them. One of the more humorous inventions was the cream jug in the shape of a cow, a joke that has remained popular ever since. In Britain, the first salt-glazed stoneware jugs of the mid-1700s copied silver examples. Later, they were made in all kinds of pottery: earthenware with lead glaze and tortoiseshell decoration, with underglaze painting and printing, enamel painting and lustres. A few were made in porcelain. Potters all over Britain made cow creamers, including in Staffordshire, Yorkshire, Tyneside, Scotland and Wales.

Dropping a live toad into someone's ale, either as a prank or for supposed medicinal benefit, may be the origin of the frog mug, a popular potters' joke. From around the 1770s they were made at potteries all over the country, but numbers from Yorkshire and Sunderland show that the jest was particularly popular in the North East. Creamware, pearlware, lustre ware and commemoratives are found with anything from a single frog to a whole crowd of frogs, toads or newts. Sometimes a rhyme would give a clue to the contents, but often the decoration, such as fine floral painting on a bone china mug, belies the surprising contents!

Victorian flatback figures

Victorian portrait figures or 'flatbacks' are so called because, being designed to stand on a mantelpiece, they have flat, undecorated backs. The potter was not going to waste time painting the parts that did not show. Flatbacks first began to appear in the late 1830s, and included a great many images of royalty, following Queen Victoria's accession in 1837. They were made by many factories throughout the 19th and into the 20th centuries, and reproductions are common. The subject range is enormous: royalty, military and historical figures, characters and events from literature and the stage, figures from religion, politics and current affairs – particularly scandal and violent crime.

❧ Group of earthenware figures on square bases: in the fashionable neoclassical style of the period. Made in Staffordshire, 1790–1810.

➤ Prince Albert and Queen Victoria with the Princess Royal: earthenware. Made in Staffordshire, about 1841.

❧ Continuing the tradition: bone china figures of Columbine and Harlequin, pattern numbers HN2185 and HN2186, designed by Peggy Davies in 1957 and made by Royal Doulton, Burslem.

19TH-CENTURY POTTERS & THEIR POTS

▲ Job Ridgway (1759–1813) by Thomas Ryles. Brothers Job and George Ridgway established their family business at the Bell Works, Shelton, Staffordshire, now the site of The Potteries Museum & Art Gallery. The Ridgways built and owned several major factories around Shelton. They were Methodists and great benefactors of the church in the Potteries.

Useful and beautiful

By the early 1800s the foundations for the enduring success of the pottery industry had been laid. Popular, reliable types of ceramics had been developed, including fine earthenware, stoneware and bone china. New ones were introduced, such as stone china in the early 1800s, upon which the huge export market and catering ware trade depended later in the century. The technology of manufacturing advanced during the century. The introduction of 'jigger' and 'jolley' machinery for shaping the wares, and methods such as transfer printing for decorating pots, encouraged greater mass-production.

The leading master potters were wealthy, influential people and many businesses established in the late 1700s and early 1800s remain well-known today. Thomas Minton founded his firm in 1796; the Ridgway family businesses operated from about 1802 and the name continued until 1964. The London china dealer Miles Mason opened his factory in Staffordshire in the early 1800s, joining many other well-established potters.

Many potteries, however, were small businesses which did not leave legacies of marked wares in great quantity, and tribute must be paid to the small manufacturers and many thousands of anonymous workers who contributed to the success of the pottery industry.

◄ Bone china bust of Josiah Spode II made at the Spode works, Stoke-upon-Trent, about 1805.

Style for the mass market

Several decorative types of pottery became popular in the 19th century because they were economical and practical as well as attractive.

Mocha ware was earthenware decorated with coloured clay slip bands, dots, trailed lines and curious tree-like patterns. It was often used in inns and wherever useful jugs, mugs and wares were required.

Lustre ware was decorative earthenware or bone china with shiny metallic effects made with metal oxides. Pink, silver and copper were the most common colours, applied overall or with patterns painted, splashed or stencilled over the glaze.

Underglaze painted pearlware was economical to produce because all the colours used could be fired together with the glaze.

◄ Earthenware teapot, moulded in the form of a castle, with a howling Dalmatian finial. Underglaze painted colours in typical shades which could be fired along with the glaze. Possibly made in Staffordshire, about 1810.

Transfer-printing, however, was the most important invention for pottery decoration. Printing in underglaze blue on earthenware was not perfected until the late 1790s, but once this happened highly decorative and economical tableware could be produced in huge quantities. Oriental patterns were popular at first, followed by views and landscapes, some specially designed for export to America. Other colours were introduced in the 1820s and 30s, and in the 1840s a way of making multicolour prints was invented.

Every pot tells a story

During the Victorian period, people liked pots to be much more than merely useful, so potters made wares with a story to tell. Making pots in moulds meant that they could be quite complicated, so scenes from mythology and literature began to appear on jugs, often made from coloured stoneware with a light glaze covering (or 'smearglaze'). Commemorative wares have been made as long as pottery itself, but the 19th century saw a massive increase in ceramic mementoes for all kinds of events and people – from royalty to a local chapel or band; all had their moment on pottery. The popularity of commemoratives has continued: to this day, the industry is always pleased to have an election, a royal wedding or birth to celebrate in ceramics.

▲ Earthenware jug with copper lustre, and printed decoration and inscription: 'Success to the Coal Trade James & Sarah Harp 1826'; probably Staffordshire, about 1826.

▼ Jug in smearglazed stoneware with relief-moulded decoration in the Gothic-revival style of the mid-19th century. The design for this 'apostle jug' was registered with the patent office by the maker, Charles Meigh, on 17 March 1842.

◄ Plate with an underglaze blue transfer-printed pattern of lions, taken from Rees's *Cyclopaedia*, published in 1807. Potters often copied illustrations from books and prints. Made by William Adams, Tunstall, Staffordshire, about 1810.

▼ View of Stoke-upon-Trent, about 1832–45, by Henry Lark Pratt.

THE ART & CRAFT OF THE POTTER

Showcase to the world

British manufacturers demonstrated their technical skill and artistry worldwide at the Great Exhibition at the Crystal Palace, Hyde Park, London, in 1851 and the many exhibitions which followed. Revivals of pottery styles of the past became all-important and were the epitome of Victorian design: 18th-century French Sevres porcelain, in particular, was frequently imitated, often with greater technical skill than the real thing. Victorian majolica, based originally on Italian Renaissance pottery, developed its own colourful character over the decades following its introduction at the 1851 exhibition.

The ornamental ware made by the great Victorian manufacturers – Minton, Copeland, Wedgwood, Doulton, Brownfield, Davenport, George Jones, Brown-Westhead, Moore & Co, and many others – may seem extravagant today. Even at the time they were not without their critics, and from the 1860s there was a reaction against the excesses of industrial production.

The Arts & Crafts movement

Some potters turned their backs on industry to pursue higher ideals of craftsmanship, after the teachings of John Ruskin, William Morris and their followers. The results were diverse: artistic, sculptural stoneware by the Martin Brothers of London; decorative pottery produced in the art studios run by Minton and Doulton, also in London; lustre wares and tiles made by William De Morgan which blend the decorative style of the Arts and Crafts movement with that of Middle Eastern and Renaissance pottery. De Morgan was a major figure in this new generation, as were other experimental art potters of the late 19th and early 20th centuries who created exciting glaze effects and experimented with oriental high-temperature firing techniques.

Bernard Moore was a Staffordshire potter who specialised in experimental work. His wares, with their random, rich colouring in copper-based reds and yellows, are amongst the most beautiful of all art pottery.

◀ Portrait of Bernard Moore (1850–1935). Formerly an industrial potter with his family firm of Moore Brothers, he turned to experimental art pottery around 1900.

▲ Bone china dessert plate decorated in the Sevres revival style, with a painted view of the Crystal Palace exhibition, London, 1851. Made by Minton & Co, Staffordshire.

▼ Garden centrepiece in earthenware with majolica decoration in the Renaissance-revival style. Made by Minton & Co, Staffordshire, 1855.

'Summer', painted by Albert Slater, from a set of 'Four Seasons' tile panels made by Minton, Hollins and Co, Staffordshire, for Longton Swimming Baths, 1886.

Teapot moulded in the form of a seated Chinaman, with coloured majolica glazes, impressed shape number 1838 and date cipher. Made by Minton & Co, Staffordshire, dated 1874.

Jardiniere: salt-glazed stoneware with incised decoration by Hannah Barlow, one of the lady artists employed at Doulton's art pottery studio at Lambeth, London. Made in 1877.

Modelled caricature fish in salt-glazed stoneware by the Martin Brothers, four brothers who made art pottery at Fulham and Southall, London, from 1873 to about 1914.

Life-size peacock, earthenware with majolica decoration, modeled by Paul Comolera. Made by Minton & Co, Staffordshire, 1873.

TILES

Decorative tiles had their heyday in Victorian Britain due to the demand for practical, hygienic and attractive surfaces. Medieval tiles inspired Gothic-revival designers, such as A.W.N. Pugin, during the 1830s–50s and new methods like mechanical tile-pressing, 'dust pressing' of dry clay powder, and transfer-printing meant that huge quantities of tiles could be produced cheaply and reliably.

Churches were furnished with tile floors, picture tile panels decorated children's hospital wards, and most Victorian public buildings had decorative encaustic tiled floors and glazed tiled walls. Picture tiles were popular, especially the many illustrative series such as those designed by William Wise and John Moyr Smith for Minton & Co in the 1870s.

William De Morgan's designs, based on Islamic tile patterns, were particularly fashionable and were imitated by the industrial tile manufacturers in Staffordshire, Shropshire, Yorkshire and Manchester. Coloured glazes, 'tube-lining' and the art nouveau style of the early 1900s were especially suited to tiles for walls and fire-surrounds.

Painted tiles by William De Morgan, London, 1890s, with design based on Islamic tiles.

A LIVING INDUSTRY

In the 1900s there was little change in pottery design at first. The swirling lines of art nouveau and the vibrant glaze colours of art pottery were adopted by industrial potters, but it was not until after the First World War and the dawn of the modern age that new, fashionable styles were seen. The success of the Staffordshire Potteries, however, was built on their production of traditional wares in shapes and patterns of the 18th and 19th centuries. In a world marketplace, these products were, and continue to be, the mainstay of the industry.

Art deco

There were different aspects to the lively, modern art deco designs of the 1920s and 30s. Best known are probably Clarice Cliff's jazzy designs, with their bright colours, abstract patterns and geometric shapes. Tableware by Susie Cooper brought modernism to a traditional industry with good, functional design and use of new decorating methods. Typical of the excellent modern productions of Wedgwood were the elegant architectural vases of Keith Murray, decorative modernist tablewares by Victor Skellern and Eric Ravilious, and stylised animals modelled by the sculptor John Skeaping. Streamlined forms and matt glazes were key features of 1930s pottery design.

Austerity and after

Restrictions on the production of decorated pottery for the home market were introduced during the Second World War and did not end until 1952. Potters took up where they had left off before the war, but a 1950s style emerged, launched by the Festival of Britain

▲ 'Inspiration' vase by Clarice Cliff in earthenware with underglaze painting; made by Newport Pottery Co Ltd, Burslem, about 1929.

➤ Earthenware vase, shape 4062, designed by Keith Murray in 1933 with matt glaze and enamel painted pattern 'Springtime', designed by Millicent Taplin in 1939. Made by Wedgwood, Barlaston, Staffordshire, 1940.

◄ Pierced bowl in earthenware, decorated with 'Shooting Star' pattern overglaze. Made by George Wade & Sons, Burslem, 1956.

◄ Coffee service, designed by Susie Cooper on 'Kestrel' shape, underglaze painted onto earthenware. Made at Wood & Sons Ltd, Burslem, and decorated at Susie Cooper Pottery, Burslem, about 1934.

▲ Coffee service in 'Totem' pattern, designed by Susan Williams-Ellis and made by Portmeirion Pottery, Stoke-on-Trent, about 1963–70.

▲ Part dinner service in 'Coral Firs' pattern on 'Biarritz' shape, printed and painted onto earthenware. Designed by Clarice Cliff and made by A.J. Wilkinson, Burslem, 1933–38.

▲ Clarence and Clara, a pair of earthenware vases from a series 'Buddies'. Made by George Wade & Sons, Burslem, 1950s.

in 1951. The streamlined theme continued but with the addition of asymmetrical shapes and patterns based on aspects of modern life, such as science, travel and contemporary interior design. Midwinter was one of the best known manufacturers and their tableware range included designs by Hugh Casson, Terence Conran and Jessie Tait.

Late 20th century and beyond

The 1960s saw strong shapes in pottery – cylinders and other geometric forms, with patterns along the same theme. Shapes continued to be strong and chunky into the 1970s, especially suitable for the new ranges of oven-to-tableware – designed so that the same dish could be used to cook food and then serve it at the table. Stoneware, and predominantly brown colours, were common: the industry's response to the popularity of studio pottery. The mug became one of the most important introductions at this time and many millions are now produced each week.

▲ Walking wares, earthenware. Designed by Danka Napiorkowska and Roger Mitchell, 1973. Made by Carlton Ware, Stoke-on-Trent.

Once demand for brown pots subsided, the industry responded with lighter, brighter wares with patterns in pastel colours. Coordination of all kinds of kitchen and dining room items became popular as retailers themed their ranges of pottery and housewares. Whatever style fashion dictates, the pottery industry responds, but its reputation depends upon well-made wares in traditional shapes and patterns.

▼ Earthenware plate with printed 'Homemaker' pattern designed by Enid Seeney, 1957, on 'Metro' shape designed by Tom Arnold, 1957. Made by Ridgway Potteries, Stoke-on-Trent, 1957–67.

Technological advances in the 20th century affected the way pottery is made and decorated. Most important was the introduction of the tunnel-oven for firing, which made bottle ovens obsolete in the industry. New decorating methods such as lithographic and silk screen printing have become widely used, but transfer-printing using paper has been kept alive, along with other traditional skills, such as hand-painting and flower-making.

STUDIO POTTERY

Pioneer studio potters

Like the potters of the Arts and Crafts movement, studio potters of the early 20th century turned their backs on industry. Chinese, Japanese and Korean ceramics, along with British pottery from the medieval period to slipware of the early 18th century, provided the main sources of inspiration.

Making pottery became a lifestyle more than a job. Studio potters would build their own wheels and kilns, fire their pots with wood they had gathered themselves, and then sell their own wares. The features of early studio pottery were that it was often round, having been thrown on the wheel, and predominantly brown, cream or green earthy colours.

Pioneering potters in the early 20th century were Bernard Leach, who established his pottery at St Ives, Cornwall, and had lived in Japan; William Staite Murray, who made large, sculptural pieces and considered himself an artist working in clay; and Denise Wren, who taught a whole generation of pottery teachers. Following in their footsteps came Shoji Hamada, a Japanese potter who worked with Leach, and Michael Cardew and Katherine Pleydell-Bouverie, who were both early pupils at the Leach Pottery.

New directions

Bernard Leach's influence was far-reaching, but in the late 1930s two potters from Europe, Lucie Rie and Hans Coper, brought sophisticated styles and techniques to British studio pottery. Lucie Rie was inspired by oriental shapes and glazes, but the influence of the modern movement in design was also strong in her work. Hans Coper produced stoneware thrown on the wheel to make sculptural pieces with textured surfaces. Both taught at the Royal College of Art, London, in the decades after the war, and the next generation of studio potters learned that experimentation and wide-ranging decorative effects were available to them. Techniques such as tin-glazing and lustre decoration were revived by Alan Caiger-Smith, and salt-glazing, used by Denise Wren, became popular with post-war studio potters.

Modern claywork

Since the 1970s, the range of clays, materials and techniques open to potters has been immense. Thrown, hand-built and slip-cast forms for sculptural or useful wares can be glazed, painted, polished, printed or decorated with firing effects. Firing can be conventional, using any fuel, or raku, using sawdust. Gone is

▲ Bowl, stoneware, yellow glaze with running bronze rim, Lucie Rie, London, about 1970.

➤ Dish with slip-trailed decoration, Bernard Leach, St Ives, Cornwall, 1921–37.

▲ 'Fountains' bowl in earthenware with slip decoration, Michael Cardew, Winchcombe, Gloucestershire, 1938.

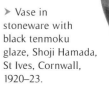

➤ Vase in stoneware with black tenmoku glaze, Shoji Hamada, St Ives, Cornwall, 1920–23.

the requirement for studio pottery to be round and brown. The combination of historical methods with modern design and technology has resulted in great diversity, ranging from useful wares for the home to sculptural works in the realms of fine art.

The Bergen Collection

In 1948 Dr Henry Bergen (1875–1950) gave his collection of pioneer studio pottery to the museum. Bergen, an American, came to Europe to study history. Already an admirer of oriental art, he met Bernard Leach following his return from Japan and took an active interest in the Leach Pottery at St Ives. Bergen collected all kinds of pottery by Leach, Hamada and their pupils. He befriended Michael Cardew and was a regular visitor at Cardew's Winchcombe Pottery in Gloucestershire. The collection is a unique record of the early years of British studio pottery as it includes experimental pieces along with successful lines, all gathered 'hot from the kiln'.

The Pinchen Collection

Robert Pinchen (1934–94) was a Yorkshireman with a passion for collecting studio pottery. His collection began on family holidays to Cornwall in the mid-1960s and he bought from the Leach Pottery among others in the county. As his interest grew, he acquired items he liked (the main criterion for his collecting) from all over the country. Not only did he buy items by established potters, but he also visited art school degree shows looking for the work of new, young potters. The Pinchen Collection complements the Bergen Collection in that it reflects the main trends in studio pottery in the late 20th century.

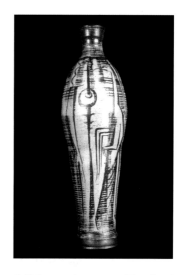

⌃ Tall vase, stoneware with painted decoration depicting 'Leda & the Swan', by Robert Washington, Chelmsford, Essex, 1981.

⌄ Earthenware vessel with matt glaze, hand-built by Gordon Baldwin, Eton, Berkshire, 1995.

◀ Female torso, raku, Jenny Rivron, York, about 1990.

▶ Porcelain dish with under- and overglaze painted decoration, Russell Coates, Somerset, 2001.

POTTERY WORDS
AND WAYS EXPLAINED

Biscuit firing The first firing of a pot which is then to be decorated and/or glazed then fired again one or more times.

Body, bodies The type of pottery from which a piece is made: mainly earthenware, porcelain or stoneware.

Ceramic The broad term for all objects made of fired clay, derived from the Greek word *keramikos* ('of pottery').

Creamware White earthenware with a tinted lead glaze giving a warm cream colour.

Earthenware Pottery made from clays which have been fired, but are only impervious to liquid when glazed; any pottery which is not stoneware or porcelain.

▲ Painting and Gilding China or Earthenware.

Enamel colours Coloured pigments, usually made from metallic oxides and glaze, used for hand-painted decoration over the glaze.

Encaustic Literally meaning 'burnt in', the term was used by Josiah Wedgwood for his painted black basalt neo-classical vases; also describes Victorian floor tiles with inlaid patterns.

Firing Heating up clay objects to high temperatures, often more than 1,000°C, to chemically change the fragile, dry material into resilient pottery .

▲ 'Glazing' or dipping the ware in a prepared liquid which produces the glofsy surface.

Glaze A layer of glass fired on to the surface of pots to make them impervious to liquid or to decorate them.

Jigger, Jolley Machines with built-in tools and moulds that produced large quantities of identical flat ware (jigger) and hollow ware (jolley) and replaced many skilled throwers.

Lead Used extensively for glazes until the danger of poisoning was recognised in the late 19th century when alternatives were found.

▲ A Potters Oven when firing or baking, the ware therein placed in Safeguards, or 'Saggers'.

Oven A kiln for firing pottery. These had distinctive bottle-shaped exteriors in Staffordshire for at least 200 years until the mid-20th century.

Overglaze Any decoration which is applied once the glaze has been fired onto the pot.

Pearlware White earthenware with a slightly blue-tinted lead glaze.

Porcelain Translucent, vitrified pottery, usually white. Variations are soft-paste (artificial), hard-paste (true), including oriental porcelain, and bone china.

▲ 'Prefsing' or 'Squeezing', which is making jugs, turenes e&c. of the clay, ready for being fired.

Pressing Making objects from sheets of clay put in a plaster of Paris mould in two or more parts which are then pressed together.

Raku A type of low-temperature fired pottery from Japan which has become popular with studio potters. The pots are often taken out of the kiln whilst still hot.

▲ Examining and drefsing the ware after its coming from the potter's and glazing ovens.

Raw materials The ingredients for making and decorating pottery: mainly china clay, ball clay, china stone, burnt and crushed flint, bone ash, and metallic oxides such as cobalt, manganese, iron, copper and even uranium for making colours.

▲ The Moddler or Sculptor, from whose productions are taken casts or moulds for the potter.

Relief moulding Any method of making a pot or separate decoration in moulds, so that the finished effect is three-dimensional rather than flat.

▲ Placing the 'dipped' ware ready for its being fired or baked in the 'Glazing' Oven.

Saggar Fireclay container into which pottery was placed to protect it during firing.

Salt-glaze A glaze formed on the surface of stoneware pots by

▲ 'Blending' or mixing the materials with water, forming a Compound called Slip.

throwing common salt into the kiln during firing.

Slip, slipware, slip-casting Clay made into a thick liquid by mixing it with water (slip), which can then be used for decorating pottery (slipware) or making pottery in moulds (slip-casting).

▲ First procefs of potting is 'Throwing', forming round pieces of ware with the Hands or Machine.

Stoneware Pottery fired to a high enough temperature to make it impervious to liquids without a glaze. It may then be glazed or left unglazed.

Throwing Making a pot by hand on the potter's wheel.

▲ Printing on thin paper, imprefsions transferred to the fired ware, and paper washed off.

Transfer-printing Decorating pottery repetitively with patterns transferred using paper or a gelatine 'bat' from an engraved, etched or punched metal plate or roller, either under or onto the glaze. Modern lithographic methods use printed images on plastic film.

Turning Trimming or decorating unfired, leather-hard pots with a

▲ Engraving designs on Copper Plates for producing the much admired 'blue printed pots', &c.

sharp tool using a horizontal lathe or potter's wheel to spin them.

▲ The Turner turning in a lathe and regulating the clay ware which the 'thrower' has formed.

Underglaze Any decoration which is applied before the glaze is put on and fired onto the pot.

▲ Packing China and Earthenware in 'Crates'.

Engravings taken from *A Representation of the Manufacturing of Earthenware*, 1827, with the captions of the original descriptions replicated.

PEOPLE OF THE POTTERIES

The fictional 'Five Towns' of Arnold Bennett's novels were based on the real Six Towns of the Potteries, a landscape which he described as 'a singular scenery of coal dust, potshards, flame and steam'. But this is only a small part of the picture. The unique landscape of the Potteries is a reflection of its rich industrial history, shaped by many generations of skilled and industrious people. Hanley, now the commercial centre of the city, Burslem, Tunstall, Stoke-upon-Trent, Fenton and Longton make up the Six Towns, from which, along with their surrounding villages, the City of Stoke-on-Trent was created in 1925.

⋀⋁ Pottery workers at the Broad Street Works of G.L. Ashworth & Brothers, Hanley, Staffordshire. Watercolours by J. Eyre, 1919.

Bottle ovens gave the Potteries its distinctive skyline and reputation for having a smoky, polluted atmosphere. With improvements in firing methods and the Clean Air Acts of the 20th century, this has changed, and few bottle ovens remain in the city today. Interest in the heritage of the industry's buildings, however, has resulted in surviving potteries and ovens being recorded and preserved.

The pottery industry has always been skill-based and creative. Although machinery was introduced for some processes, potting remained relatively unmechanised until recently and a number of traditional skills remain, complemented by technical, research and engineering personnel, in addition to managers and retail staff.

There are many aspects of work and life in the Potteries which have changed significantly. Health has improved through recognition of the dangers of widespread use of poisonous materials such as lead. Employment conditions, mostly good compared to those in other industries, improved steadily from the first half of the 19th century, due partly to the activities of the workers' trade unions as well as government legislation. No longer are employees paid 'good from oven' (that is, only for those items which survived the whole production process), nor are they paid in 'truck' with goods in kind. Children under 16, who throughout

⋁ Panorama of Burslem, by Reginald G. Haggar, 1940.